Pareidolia -Feb/March 2022

By Honey Beez
Copyright © 2022

ISBN: 9798363126321
Photos by pixabay.com

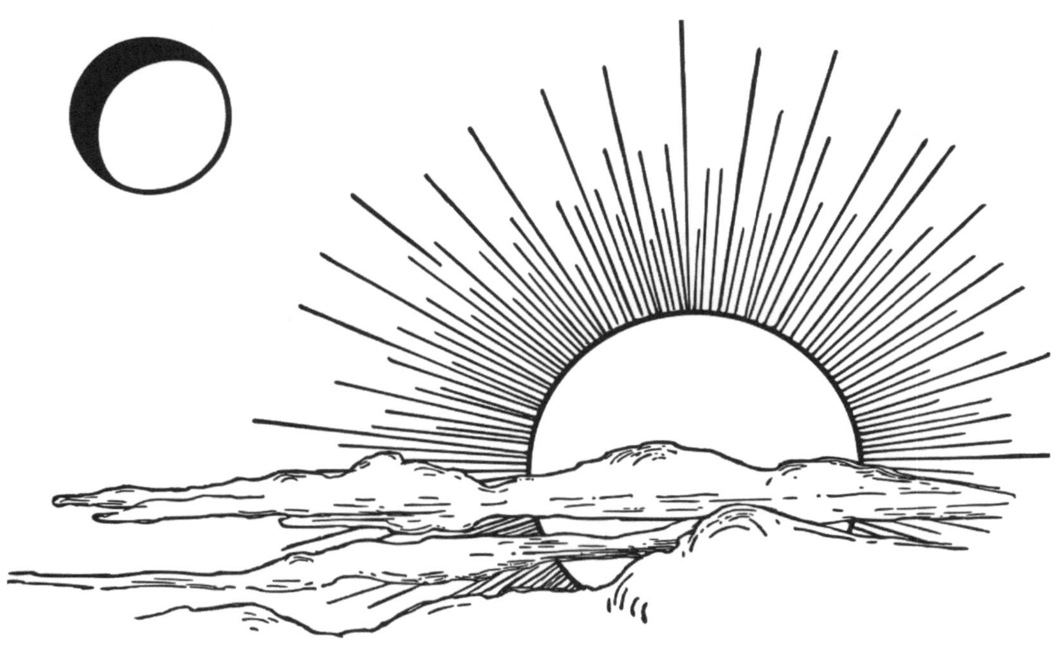

DEDICATION

This book is dedicated to my King, children and family. Also to mentally ill people and suicidal people.

CONTENTS

Pareidolia

I'm schizophrenic. Pareidolia is a common tendency for everybody, the ability to see faces or eyes in regular objects. For me, I see faces and eyes in ordinary things. Possibly it is delusional but sometimes other people can clearly see them too, like this face on the table.

I wasn't always like this, seeing things in things. Sometimes I see birds or planes fly in the sky and I believe they are from God. In the Bible there are several passages that say "Seek His face" or something like that and for me I can seek is face in like stucco or patterns and a face will appear and it is like God saying "Hi".

I frequently see an eye or eyes in cloud formations :)

Sometimes a house can look like two eyes or a face.

These little reminders to me are like from God saying "hello"!

Hidden Messages in Music

The following are over a thousand songs that I have collected in the link:

Here is all the playlists on youtube:
https://www.youtube.com/channel/UCHmF1LRK AQOn9LN_-w-R-uw/playlists

It has happened where I can hear a hidden message in music. Sometimes a voice or a word can come from sounds with the way I interrupt it I guess. I happens to me less now really this is just a music playlist of music I like now.

Some themes of music you may find in my songs are: positivity, light, the sun, the name Honey, bees, God and birds.

YouTube deletes videos all the time and I lose songs. So I make these books to list the song titles so I can look them up again so I can recreate my playlists.

Feb/March 2022

Here is the playlist link corresponding to this book:
https://www.youtube.com/playlist?list=PLHV3RYKvGS65XpI7bRED6Kksjje9jODU_

Hybrid Minds BBC Radio 1 Essential Mix 29.08.20

Fred V - Trust Me (ft. SAYAH)

Hybrid Minds - Inside (ft. Emily Jones)

[DnB] - Feint - Snake Eyes (feat. CoMa) [Monstercat Release]

Etherwood - I Will Wave To You

Hospital Records Drum & Bass Mix - 2017 Year Mix

Hospital Records Vocal Drum & Bass Mix 2018

Logistics - Secret Satellite (feat. Zoë Phillips)

HIGH CONTRAST | Music Please at Roxy Prague

Kanye West Sunday Service - "hallelujah, salvation, and glory" (Live From Paris, France)

2021-03-28 H25PITAL - Celebrating 25 years of Hospital Records -Offbeatdooter

Voltage - Save Me From Myself (Harriet Jaxxon Remix)

Hospital Podcast 227 with London Elektricity - Heaven Special

Water In Your Veins -Etherwood

Keeno - Lifeline (feat. Oscar Corney)

Fred V & Grafix - Shaded

Royalston - Days Go On (feat. Bianca Calandra)

Etherwood - Swans (feat. Sigrún Stella)

Chris Tomlin - Good Good Father (Audio)

Mujhe Teri Mohabbat Ka FULL SONG (मुझे तेरी मोहब्बत का सहारा मिल गया होता) -Rajendra Kumar - Sadhana

Freedom (Sub Focus & Wilkinson)

Sub Focus & Wilkinson (feat. Empara Mi) - Freedom (Sub Focus & Wilkinson & High Contrast Remix)

Polar Youth ft. Georgie Allen - All Night (Metrik Remix)

Anchorman - afternoon delight scene

Logistics - Pleasure

Congo Natty Junglist

Sef Kombo b2b Kitty Amor Afro House DJ Set From DJ Mag HQ

Buku - Front To Back (Bassnectar Remix)

K Motionz - Tell You

Dua Lipa - Homesick (Netsky Bootleg) [WARNER UK]

UK APACHI With SHY FX - Original Nuttah

Natalie Imbruglia "Smoke" (GANJA KRU MIX 1) HQ

SOLAH - Fly

Georgie Riot - Take Over (ft. OHKAY)

Sub Focus, Wilkinson - Illuminate (Tour Video)

Lauren Daigle Top 20 Christian Worship Songs 2020 Nonstop Praise & Worship Songs 2020

Муслим МАГОМАЕВ "Синяя вечность"

Муслим Магомаев "Ноктюрн" (1988)

London Grammar - If You Wait (Calibre Alternate Remix)

Camo & Krooked (DJ Set), Live From A Wind Turbine - UKF On Air

Wilkinson & Becky Hill - Here For You

We're still the kids we used to be | Ghost Town by Kanye featuring 070 Shake

Netsky & Hybrid Minds - Let Me Hold You

Nightingale -Logistics

Motion Blur (NickBee Remix)

Camo & Krooked - UKF On Air in the Alps (DJ Set)

HOLY SPIRIT RIVER | Two hours of instrumental music and water sounds for stress relief

Technimatic - Goodbye Kiss

Grafix - Hospitality Park Warm Up - Mix Sessions 002

Monster Mash

Dynamite MC - Deep Water (feat. Royalston)

Hybrid Minds - Liquicity Winterfestival 2017

Hybrid Minds D&B DJ Set Live From Their Home

Lata Mangeshkar - Ehsan Tera Hoga - Junglee

Tom Walker - Just You And I (Hybrid Minds Remix)

Johannes Bornlof ft Le June Monsoons Fred V Bootleg UPDATED

Flume ft. Vera Blue - Rushing Back (Ekko & Sidetrack Bootleg)

Golden Slumbers / Carry That Weight / The End -Beatles

Netsky [GLASSHOUSE] New Zealand - UKF On Air (DJ Set)

Keys N Krates ft. Ambré Perkins - Glitter (Netsky Remix)

Dimension - Remedy (ft. TS Graye)

Best of Hybrid Minds: Artist Liquid Drum and Bass Mix #8

Bcee - Lost & Found (Hybrid Minds Remix)

Grafix x Lee Mvtthews - Underground (ft. Elipsa)

Diplo - Florida - Florida

Nu:Tone BBC Radio One Essential Mix - 31/07/2021

Logistics - Vega (Official Video)

Unglued - Sunbathing In Space

Fred V - Icarus (Official Video)

Future Symptoms B2B2B (Hub Mix Series)

Tu Tu Tu Tu Tara - Bol Radha Bol | Kumar Sanu, Poornima | Juhi Chawla & Rishi Kapoor

Hospital Mixtape: Lens Minimix

Lens - Winter Warmer Mix

Scorpions - Shining of your soul - new single Rock Believer album 2022

Rockin' Robin-Bobby Day

GEST, Quadrant & Iris - Sequential

Flava D - Classic Symptoms Mix

Hospital Podcast 452 with Whiney

Hospital Podcast 453 with Chris Goss & Degs - Forza Horizon Special

JAY-Z - Lost One ft. Chrisette Michele

Hospital Podcast 441 with Hugh Hardie

Hospital Podcast 425 Grafix Takeover

Wilkinson - Used To This (ft. Issey Cross)

Apashe - Distance (feat. Geoffroy)

Abba - Honey, Honey (1976)

Nu:Tone - Sweeter

Hospital Records Podcast 360 with Logistics

TEARS FOR FEARS ♤◇◇◇ I KNOW THIS MUCH IS TRUE

Fred V & Grafix Hospital Records Drum & Bass Mix

Mitekiss - Embers (ft. Ruth Corey)

Jelena Karleusa - Ne smem da se zaljubim u tebe [feat. Sasa Matic]

MUZZ - Spectrum (Futurebound Remix)

ODESZA - All We Need (feat. Shy Girls)

DJ Fresh - 'Gold Dust' (Official Video)

Diplo & RY X - Your Eyes (Official Full Stream)

Friction - Believer

DROELOE - A Day With Bitbird (2020 Set)

ODESZA VIBES III - EVENING CHILL MIX (new music)

Odesza Inspired Sun Mix

Harvest | A Odesza Mix By ASAHN

Mitekiss - Bolson

Bensley - Leaving

New Kids On The Block - Bring Back The Time (Ft Salt-N-Pepa, Rick Astley, En Vogue) (Official Video)

Harry Styles - Watermelon Sugar (Official Audio)

Casting Crowns - Oh My Soul (Official Lyric Video)

Lally x Lens - Love The Way

WHATUPRG - Glory feat. GAWVI

Netsky Essential Mix BBC Radio 1 [REUPLOAD]

SubFocus - Essential Mix

pendulum: girl in the fire

Flite - Blue Spark VIP

Voltage & Nicky Blackmarket - Jazz Tickles

Fred V & Grafix - Like The Sun (Official Video)

Grafix - Feel Alive (feat. Lauren L'aimant)

Fred V & Grafix - Here With You feat Collin McLoughlin

Alias - More Than Words Can Say(with lyrics)

Axel Thesleff - Need You

Hugh Hardie - Got U Wrong (feat. Phaction & Javeon)

Gotta Live - Tedashii Ft Jordan Feliz [Lyric Video]

Hospital Podcast 432 - Nu:Tone Takeover

Dusty Springfield / Windmills Of Your Mind

Must hear!! Davy Spillane - Caoineadh Cu Chulainn Uilleann Pipes.flv

Ashley MacIsaac - Sleepy Maggie

Etherwood 'Neon Dust' Film

Bailey ft Jodie Connor - Higher State 2012 (Radio Edit)

Soni Soni Full Holi Song in HD Mohabbatein

Keeno & Whiney Drum & Bass Mix - Hospital Records & Med School Mix

Makoto - Ascender

Infected Mushroom - The Messenger

Makoto History Set @ 0 Zero

Goya Menor, Nektunez – Ameno Amapiano Remix (you want to bamba, you want to chill with the big boys)

Nyan Cat 10 hours HD 1080p

High Contrast - Questions (ft. Boy Matthews)

Mr. Williamz - Sound Killa, Pt. 2 (ft. Shy FX & Specialist Moss)

Hospital Podcast 430 - Keeno Takeover

Camo & Krooked - Loa (Fade Black Remix)

(09) McKinney's Cotton Pickers - I Want a Little Girl

Fred V & Grafix - Altitude (feat. Amy J Pryce)

Chingis Khaan- Batzorig Vaanchig

Pirapus & 33 Below - Slipping Away

Hardwell LIVE at Ultra Music Festival
Miami 2022

Camo & Krooked - Loa (Fade Black Remix)

Unglued - Way Back When (feat. Esther
Durin) (Halogenix Remix)

Ty Brasel - "The Power" feat. KB (Official
Music Video)

for KING & COUNTRY - For God Is With Us
(Official Music Video)

Lecrae - Holupwait

Hulvey, KB, Lecrae - Can't Tell It All
(Remix) (Official Audio)

Chase & Status - BBC Radio 1 Essential
Mix 03.11.18

NETSKY BBC Radio 1 - ESSENTIAL MIX - Feb 2015.

ABOUT THE AUTHOR

Honey is a retired computer hacker, mother, and avid chess addict.   Honey is an American and a New Yorker. She also created a chess opening described in her book: "The Bee Defense", available on Amazon.com, which is part of a book series called "The Bee Defense". She also authored a book series to help kids with computer science topics called "Baby Blackhat". She has authored many short stories as well.

Website: https://beedefense.net

Twitter: @HoneyBeez0x

Facebook: https://www.facebook.com/honey0x

Amazon: https://www.amazon.com/Honey-Beez/e/B08ODJWJON

Merch: https://streamlabs.com/honey0x/merch